Granny Rabbit's Gooseberry Pie

Stories and Poems

Mayna Cosby Parks

Granny Rabbit's Gooseberry Pie: Stories and Poems

Copyright 2017 Mayna Cosby Parks

Illustrations by Ryan Hammett

ISBN 978-1-940645-49-0

COURIER PUBLISHING

PUBLISHED IN THE UNITED STATES OF AMERICA

Dedicated to our great-grandchildren:
Devin Lavigne, Clair Parks, Eavan Parks,
Harper Parks, Grayson Parks

And other children:
Lucille Warner, Eden Grace Giordano, Lucy Austin

In loving memory of my husband,
Marion Brooks Parks, Sr.
August 8, 1932 - May 12, 2016
Our marriage was but for a few years,
But we shared a lifetime of love.

My sincere thanks to Shirley Fogle and Denise Huffman.

Foreword

My poetic wings are little more than pinfeathers. There are innumerable reservoirs of required study, hard rules and regulations concerning the craft of poetry; unfortunately, I have not been made privy to any of them. Because of this, I confess to being a "poetic heretic." But when God gives you the desire to write, you must write above your ignorance and in Him, let your soul and spirit, without encumbrance, soar upward toward the light. *"In Him was life and that life was the light of men" (John 1:4, NIV).*

I have borrowed liberally from Matthew Henry, John MacArthur and John L. Rice.

When I have asked the reader to look into his heart, I have done so and have found myself wanting.

Mayna Cosby Parks
October 2017

P.S. I offer this small piece of advice for would-be writers of poetry: It is best to begin writing before the age of eighty-five.

Table of Contents

Stories and Such

Granny Rabbit's Gooseberry Pie

Old Granny Rabbit leaned far out of her kitchen window and shouted sternly, "Stop, thief! Come back here with my gooseberry pie!"

But the swiftly moving little figure had already bounced out of sight. Granny twitched her nose furiously and scratched her ear in disbelief.

"That's the third gooseberry pie I've lost in three weeks!" she exclaimed.

The next day, Granny Rabbit had a plan for catching the rascal who had stolen her three pies. She made another gooseberry pie and placed precisely in the center of it a piece of green she had shaved right out of the rainbow, while it rested one day in her back yard after a lazy shower.

With a twitch of her nose, Granny Rabbit placed the pie in her oven. Shortly, there arose the wonderful fragrance of wild gooseberries, fresh cinnamon, and rainbow green. It filled Mrs. Rabbit's house and floated outdoors beyond the woods and meadows.

When the pie bubbled and the crust cracked with a buttery-brown and sugary goodness, Granny Rabbit carefully took it from the oven and set it gently in the window to cool.

"Oh, my!" she whispered almost reverently as she watched a little green rainbow arch itself like a handle over the delicious-smelling pie.

In a short while, just as Granny Rabbit had expected, the pie disappeared from the windowsill.

The next morning, there was a knock on Granny Rabbit's door. Opening it, she saw a very sad Fluffy Cottontail. His whiskers trembled, his droopy ears pointed in different directions and a pale green glowed about them.

"I ate your pies all up," admitted Fluffy, hanging his head. "But I can make it up to you," he added hopefully.

Granny Rabbit looked sternly down her glasses, twitched her nose rapidly, and said, "Indeed you will!" She led Fluffy to the gooseberry patch, gave him a pail, and seated herself in the cool shade while he picked gooseberries in the hot sun.

Then together they made another pie just as luscious as the last ones.

Cutting herself a large wedge, Granny Rabbit ate it while Fluffy watched enviously. But he remembered that he had eaten four pies while she'd had none.

"That's so good," Granny exclaimed, "that I could almost eat another piece," and with that she cut an even larger slice than before.

Fluffy thought, "Oh, no! I can't watch her eat another piece!" But the pie was set down right in front of him! "I don't deserve it," Fluffy sighed.

"Yes, Fluffy, you do," said Mrs. Rabbit, smiling, "for you helped to make this one. And from now on, you can help me bake my pies every Saturday — and then you can eat all you want."

Fluffy took a big bite and smiled a splendid smile full of gooseberries.

And then a curious thing happened: A little green rainbow that had been resting lightly on the tips of his ears slowly flew up, hovered momentarily, and then floated lazily out of the window and disappeared into the glittering sunlight.

Granny knew the special magic of rainbow green — it pricked the consciences of naughty rabbits!

Molly's Un-Birthday Present

"Molly," said Mommy softly, "Daddy and I have a present for you."

"Is it my birthday?" asked Molly, looking up from her pillow.

"No," said Daddy, "it's not your birthday. You have the flu and don't feel well. Mommy and I want to give you something to cheer you up."

Molly sat up while Mommy propped the pillow behind her.

Daddy took something from behind his back. It was a tiny package wrapped in pink paper and tied with green ribbon.

"Open it," said Mommy.

Molly opened the box carefully. There in the box was a gold ring with a green stone that shone like a cat's eye at night.

Molly put the ring on her finger. She thought it was the prettiest thing that she had ever seen.

"Is the ring too small?" Mommy asked.

"No," Molly said, "this is the right size for me."

The next morning, Molly ate a little of her warm cereal, but she could not take her eyes off the ring. She could hardly wait to get well. She wanted to show the ring to Tina, her special friend.

Mommy came for the breakfast tray. She gave Molly her medicine. When she saw the ring on Molly's finger, Mommy frowned.

"Molly," Mommy said, "this ring is too small. We will get you another ring — one that fits."

"No," Molly said, "this is the right size for me." And she put her hand under the covers so that Mommy could not see.

"I'll be back," Mommy said, taking Molly's tray.

When Mommy came back, she brought a bowl of water with ice cubes and soap in it. She put Molly's hand in the cold water. Molly shivered. Mommy soaped her hand. Then she tried to slide the ring off. But the ring would not come off! Mommy looked worried.

"See," Molly whispered, "the ring wants to stay on my finger. This is the right size for me."

Molly looked at her new ring. How it shone! It made her finger feel like ginger ale. She put her hand under her pillow and went to sleep.

When Molly awakened, she heard Mommy talking to Mr. Keen on the telephone. Mr. Keen lived next door and worked in a jewelry store.

"I'm afraid the ring is too small," said Mommy, "and will have to be cut off." Mommy listened. Then she thanked Mr. Keen and hung up. Molly began to cry.

"Don't cry," Mommy said, "we'll get you another ring that fits."

But Molly did not stop crying. She cried and cried until she fell asleep.

Soon Mommy came with some soup. Molly's large eyes were red and puffy.

"I don't want any soup," Molly said. "I hate soup!"

"Really?" said Mommy. "I thought you liked soup. Do you still feel badly about the ring? Don't forget that I promised you another one."

"Please, Mommy, please!" cried Molly. "Please don't let Mr. Keen cut it off."

"I'm sorry, Molly, but we must. Your finger needs room to grow."

But Molly had already pulled the cover over her head and had begun to cry again. Molly felt Mommy's touch. "You'll feel better after a while," she said.

But Molly did not feel better after a while. She cried until her eyes were swollen and her face spotted.

Later, Mommy brought some custard. Molly did not cry now. She looked like a floppy doll that had wound down.

"You'll like this," said Mommy. Molly's eyes were open but she did not look at anything.

"Can you sit up?" Mommy whispered. But Molly was as quiet as a caterpillar in a cocoon and did not move at all.

When Mr. Keen came, Molly was asleep. He saw the dried tears on her cheeks. He did not awaken her. Mommy took Molly's hand from beneath the covers. Mr. Keen slipped a hook under the ring and turned a wheel. Off came the ring.

When Molly awakened, she called for Mommy to come in a hurry. "Where is my pretty ring?" Molly asked. She was smiling! Mommy could not believe her eyes. Was this the same Molly who had cried and cried all day?

"My pretty ring is lost!" Molly cried. "But look, Mommy, look! I didn't lose my beautiful finger!"

Mommy blinked. She looked puzzled. Then she understood.

"Molly," Mommy said, kneeling down beside her, "did you think that Mr. Keen was going to cut off your finger? Is that what you thought? We would never let that happen," Mommy said, kissing Molly's finger.

Just then, Daddy walked in. He kissed Mommy and then Molly. "And how are you feeling?" asked Daddy.

"Look, Daddy," said Molly, her eyes bright. "I lost my pretty ring and found my beautiful finger!"

Daddy reached into his pocket and took something out. It was a ring. It was a gold ring with a green stone that shone like a cat's eye at night.

Daddy slipped it on Molly's finger.

"This ring is not too little," said Daddy.

"And this ring is not too big," said Mommy.

"This ring is really just right," said Molly, laughing.

And her eyes shone — even brighter than the ring.

And What Can Be the Use of Him?

Mark Matthews trudged slowly toward the ball field. The morning sun was bright, and his shadow loitered along on the pavement behind him.

"Get lost!" Mark said to his shadow. "I don't want anyone ever following me again." The shadow lingered, casting a gray copycat outline of his dark curly hair and slender build.

"Get away!" said Mark again, his blue eyes flashing. "You're as bad as my little brother, Jamie, tagging behind me everywhere I go."

Mark was still angry. All week he had to take care of five-year-old Jamie while Mother cared for his sick grandmother.

He was rid of Jamie now, Mark thought, but he was still being followed! He stopped and looked around. No one was looking. He jumped at his shadow, but it jumped away quickly. He leaped at its middle, but it leaped nimbly aside.

"Listen," Mark warned, "STOP FOLLOWING ME!"

Then he heard a soft ripping sound and felt a little prickle around his heels. His shadow had torn away! He watched as it wobbled slowly over the side of the road into a shallow ditch. It lay there in a shivering ball like a lonely gray puppy.

Mark's mouth fell open in surprise. But he said, "Good riddance!" and hurried on down the street.

Soon, however, he slowed down. It felt strange without a shadow. But that was silly! "What good is an old gray blob of shadow anyway?" thought Mark.

But somehow it reminded him of the accident a few days ago. Jamie had skinned his knee and wouldn't hush. When Mark reached for the cookies, he had accidentally knocked over Mother's bowl of glass fruit. Two pieces had broken! If Jamie hadn't cried, Mark reasoned, he wouldn't have had the mishap. So he told Mother that Jamie had broken the fruit.

Suddenly, Mark didn't feel like playing ball. He threw some dirt clods and then went home. After washing his hands, he looked for his dog, Lulabell.

He found her curled up, snoozing on his bedside rug, snoring quietly. Except for her freckled nose, she looked like a big swirl of vanilla ice cream.

"Mark Matthews," Mother called, "please come here!"

Mark followed her voice into the bathroom.

"Just look at this towel!" Mother said.

Mark looked and saw a big gray blob centered on the yellow towel.

"Next time, wash with soap!" said Mother over her shoulder.

Mark could not believe his eyes. His shadow had followed him home. It shimmered softly — and seemed to be mocking him! He quickly stuffed the towel into the clothes hamper.

Back in his room, Mark built a tower, but it soon grew too tall and crashed to the floor. Lulabell hobbled out to find a quieter place.

Mark's second tower was growing steadily when Mother's voice interrupted him. "Come see Lulabell," she called in a puzzled tone. Mark hurried into the den.

"Look at this dirty gray spot on her back," said Mother. "Wherever could it have come from?"

Outside, Mark soaped and scrubbed Lulabell. But when she dried — the gray blob was still there! It shimmered as before, and Mark felt sure that it was gloating. His shadow was getting even!

Mark slipped Lulabell into his room. "Get away, gray blob," he said. And poof! The shadow disappeared from Lulabell's back.

"It's gone!" Mark said, happily hugging Lulabell.

Then suddenly the sunshiny day turned dark. Mark ran to the window. How strange! The sun was still shining. Shadows jiggled on the grass. But how dark it was!

Mark raced to the mirror. "Not again!" he exclaimed. His tanned face had turned a dingy gray. The blob covered his entire head like a ghostly sack.

Before he could think, Mother came in to inspect Lulabell. "She looks beautiful!" she said.

Then she looked at Mark. "What's wrong?" she asked. "Your color isn't right. Crawl in bed right now." And she folded back the covers.

Mark was almost in tears. The shadow was ruining his life! "Let's talk later, Mom," Mark said.

"Good," said Mother.

Mark lay there and thought. Finally, he realized that the shadow was not the real problem. "My conscience is hurting me," Mark admitted to himself.

Soon Mother returned. "Ready for our talk?" she asked, smiling.

And quickly Mark blurted out the truth. "I broke the glass fruit, Mom, not Jamie!"

"I know," said Mother quietly.

"You knew!" Mark was surprised. "But how?"

"No special way," said Mother.

"But why didn't you say something?"

"I trust you, Mark, to let your conscience be your guide. I believed you would."

Then Mark told his mother about the shadow and the gray blob. "Do you believe me, Mom?"

"Well, the gray blob looked like dirt to me, and you looked sick," said Mother. "But, yes, Mark, I believe that you saw it differently."

Mark's normal color had returned, and he felt greatly relieved.

The next morning, he apologized to Jamie and earned the money to replace the broken fruit.

That afternoon, Mark hurried toward the ball field. The sun was bright, and his shadow bobbed along in front of him like a friendly guide.

"Let your conscience be your guide," Mark thought. And then he understood. "Why, you've acted as my conscience!" he said to his shadow. "You pestered me until I told the truth!"

Suddenly, Mark felt gloriously free, and he bounded with his shadow down the road. "Thank you, shadow," he whispered.

He was almost sure he heard a small voice answer, "You're welcome, Mark." He clearly saw his shadow running before him, jumping and leaping, leading him down the straight road.

Danny Dinkler's Runaway Day

Danny Dinkler was tired of doing his chores. He was tired of never having time to play. He pushed back the mop of red hair that fell over his freckled forehead and thought.

"We'll run away!" Danny said to his dog, Peanut. "Then I'll never have to do another chore."

"Woof! Woof!" Peanut barked happily as they bounded upstairs to pack.

Danny found his swimsuit and underwater goggles, a clean shirt, his roller skates and a blanket. But his suitcase was nowhere to be found.

Danny had an idea. "You can wear my things for me, Peanut." So Danny tried to put his swimsuit on Peanut. Peanut was so happy that he kicked his feet about wildly and tried twice to crawl into the bedsprings. Finally, Danny got the swimsuit on him, backwards, so that his tail would have a place to go.

"Fits perfectly!" said Danny.

Then Danny helped Peanut put on the shirt. This time, Peanut folded his paws tightly across his chest. And when Danny held up the goggles, Peanut stuck his head in the bottom dresser drawer. But at last Danny coaxed him into them.

Next, Danny tied his roller skates on Peanut's feet and secured the blanket on his back.

Then Danny took his sixty-three cents from his piggy bank and slipped it into his pocket.

"We'll ride the bus out of town," Danny told Peanut, "and watch for a good campsite."

"Woof!" Peanut agreed.

So down the stairs they went, down the walk and out onto Oak Street toward town and the bus station.

Danny felt wonderfully free and so did Peanut, especially in the behind part with the roller skates. That part was getting so far ahead of the front that it was hard to tell which end was doing the thinking.

Soon, Danny saw his grandmother.

"Hello," said Grandmother Dinkler. "Where are you going?"

"I'm running away from home," said Danny.

"That's nice," said his grandmother. "Come inside. I've just made some fudgie-wudgies."

Danny ate six of the chewy cookies and slipped two under the table for Peanut. Grandmother Dinkler didn't notice and slipped Peanut two more.

Soon, Danny told his grandmother goodbye, and he and Peanut set out down Oak Street again. "We'll be on that bus in no time," Danny told Peanut.

"Hello! Where are you going?" a voice called. It was Cindy Tupper, Danny's school friend.

"I'm running away from home," said Danny.

"That's nice," said Cindy. "Come see the robot I got for my birthday."

So Danny left Peanut and followed Cindy inside. The robot scooted back and forth with its red lights flashing.

Then Cindy's mother came home. "Cindy," she called, "please help me unload the car."

Afterwards, Mrs. Tupper made them a strawberry soda. She even gave one to Peanut!

When they finished, Danny and Peanut set out down Oak Street again. "We'll be on that bus in no time," Danny told Peanut.

By this time, Peanut was skating expertly. He zoomed back and forth, up and down the sidewalk on one hind leg, showing off.

"Hello! Where are you going?" shouted Billy Hoover, Danny's best friend.

"I'm running away from home," said Danny.

"That's nice," said Billy, "but come and see my tree house." So Danny climbed the tree with Billy.

"This room is where the secret club will meet," said Billy. "I'm going to paint the sleeping quarters now," he added, opening a can of purple paint.

"What can I do?" asked Danny.

"Just watch," said Billy. "I want to do this all by myself."

Then Danny remembered he was running away. "I have to go now," he told Billy as he climbed down the tree.

"Where are you going?" called Billy's mother from the porch.

"I'm running away from home," said Danny.

"That's nice," said Mrs. Hoover. "Call Billy. I have a surprise for both of you."

Mrs. Hoover gave them each a dish of raspberry crunch. It stuck in Peanut's teeth, and he grinned and smacked with his mouth open.

"Yuck!" said Mrs. Hoover as Peanut's tongue sloshed about like a pink mop.

Soon, Danny and Peanut set out down Oak Street again. "We'll be on that bus in no time," Danny told Peanut.

And sure enough, soon they were at the bus station. One big bus stood trembling noisily. Several people boarded, but Danny didn't see any animals get on. Quickly, he wrapped Peanut in the blanket. "Now you're my little brother, Peanut Dinkler," said Danny. "I'll do the talking."

Danny tucked the tip of Peanut's tail and a speck of his brown nose inside the blanket. Then he climbed the steep steps.

"Hello," said the driver, "where are you going?"

"My little brother and I are running away," said Danny.

"That's nice," said the driver. "How far are you going?"

Danny stuck his hand deep inside his pocket and pulled out his sixty-three cents. "This far," he said, holding out his money.

"How old is your little brother?" asked the driver.

"He's one year old," Danny said.

Just then Peanut's head pushed out of the blanket, and he peeped curiously through his goggles at the driver.

"He sure is a funny-looking little rascal," said the driver, shaking his head.

"Woof! Woof!" said Peanut.

"My! What a cough," said the driver. "Better get him to a doctor," and he handed back Danny's sixty-three cents.

Danny climbed down the steps with Peanut. The big bus moved slowly out and rumbled down the street. Danny's and Peanut's stomachs rumbled, too.

Across the street Danny spotted Miss Allred, his teacher. "Hello, Miss Allred," called Danny. "Where are you going?"

"Home," she said.

"That's nice," said Danny. "May we ride with you?"

"Hop in," said Miss Allred, and away they went.

Soon, Miss Allred stopped. She was back in a minute with two hot cherry fritters. "Enjoy these," she said.

Danny and Peanut looked at each other. As they ate, their stomachs rumbled loudly. Miss Allred thought the noise was coming from inside her car. "Something terrible is going on in the engine," she said.

Soon she pulled up in front of Danny's house and they tumbled out.

Danny undressed Peanut on the front lawn. When he took off the roller skates, Peanut showed his appreciation by doing two cartwheels and a triple somersault. Then he danced around the house on his front paws.

Danny picked up his toys that were scattered over the lawn. He emptied the garbage and put away his father's tools. He cleaned his room.

Then he and Peanut climbed into bed. Soon Danny's mother came in. "Would you two care for some fudgie-wudgies?" she asked.

Danny groaned.

Peanut whined softly and put his paws over his eyes.

"I sure did learn something today," said Danny.

"And what is that?" asked his mother.

"Running away is the hardest chore of all!" said Danny.

"Woof! Woof!" agreed Peanut.

She Drives Me Wild

My name is Constance Ann, but — naturally — they call me Connie. I have chestnut hair and six or eight freckles — and if I am to believe anyone, I should spend the rest of my life in a magazine touting toothpaste.

But not me. I love horses, stunt riding, daredevil adventure, and corn-on-the-cob — in that order. My trophies would fill a museum, or so says my dad.

I am from a little town in the South — and to my barely sixteen-year-old cousin Angela, this is a crime. At least it was, until last summer, when I introduced her to Wilton Calhoun. Now she is quietly hysterical to visit me again.

"After I visit you in New York City," I said with determination, "you will be welcome to visit me again."

Angela just stared at me coolly with these green, almond-shaped eyes, tossed her blond hair, and deliberately withheld the invitation. She drives me wild! I have seen a turtle crossing a dirt road with more commitment. One day …

Finally, the invitation came from Angela's parents, who were leaving suddenly for a trip. It was June the 11th — my thirteenth birthday. In less than two hours, I was packed and confirmed on the next flight to New York. I arrived Sunday at 1:28 a.m. in the rain, and by 8:00 a.m. I was dressed and ecstatic to the see the city.

Angela refused to get out of bed until, luckily, I found a cracked bowl and accidentally dropped it off the refrigerator into the kitchen sink. "Angela," I screamed, "I will only be here for three days!"

"I thought it was three years," she mumbled, throwing herself across the kitchen table with her coffee mug teetering at forty-five degrees. It took me an hour and a half to get her dressed, after which she consented to go window shopping. Window shopping! I had never seen the Empire State Building! Like I said, Angela drives me absolutely wild.

"Ready, Duck?" Angela asked, picking up her purse and umbrella.

As we set out from the Upper East Side toward the city, apartments and people and even the leaves on the trees jumped out at me with their subtle or striking differences from home.

Rain pelted the streets, and distant thunder grumbled in a northern key. Timid flashes of lightning gave Angela an unfamiliar look as we sped along into the city. Suddenly, I was surrounded by tall buildings that grew up like giant tombstones out of an asphalt canyon. From a colorless sky, silver droplets swirled from dizzying heights. I had never in my life felt more elated or more insignificant.

Angela veered in and out of the light traffic and came so close to a parked truck that the word Otis scratched my eyelids. She parked the car, reached for her umbrella, and we stepped out. The rain fell furiously, and we ducked under the framework of a large department store that was having a facelift.

Peering inside, I could see through the twilight sparkling chandeliers and miles of twisted lime silk draped decoratively, looking like frozen sherbet.

Leaning slightly on one of the double doors, I found it open and walked into the foyer.

"The alarm could sound," Angela cautioned with a little more vitality than usual — and just to annoy her, I pretended to push through the second set of doors. To my real amazement, the doors swung open, and I walked in, nonchalantly, just to let Angela know that I did not take orders from her. My feet sank into the spongy carpet, and I sniffed the smells of perfumes, plaids and purses. There was a bustling silence.

Inside, I waved and made faces at Angela and was delighted to see how she stared helplessly when I ignored her motions and calls to come out. Without actually planning it, I paraded down the aisle to the elevator and pressed the button. Angela was stalking me now. As the elevator door opened, she grabbed my arm, forcing my decision — and I dragged her in with me, while quickly pressing the second floor button. Angela tried to catch the door, but it was too late. She was dumbfounded.

"You wanted to window-shop," I said blithely, "so let's do it from the inside." I knew that I was being outrageous, but, like a runaway horse, I could not be stopped.

The elevator whirred strangely as Angela continued her grip on my arm. I was beginning to think that I had carried the joke too far and wondered how I was going to squeeze out gracefully when the sixth floor light blinked on. The sixth floor! The elevator stopped abruptly, but the door remained closed.

Angela and I looked at each other. She quickly pressed another button and then another. The stillness trembled. I held my breath and waited for Angela to say, "See what you have done!" She didn't, and if I hadn't been so frightened, I could have hugged her.

"The overhead light is on, so the power must still be on," Angela reasoned. We pressed the emergency button and all the others in various combinations. I could not believe what was happening. There was a prickly sensation above my lip, and my heart was running like a frightened rabbit.

Angela climbed on my shoulders and examined every inch of the ceiling. Nothing! Next, we scrutinized the floor and found no shred of hope for an escape. Tiny pinpoints of moisture glistened on Angela's forehead.

I closed my eyes. How I longed to be home on the back of Golden Mane, gliding silently through delicious, sun-drenched days, through waving wheat fields gleaming under the brilliant blue morning sky.

But I was caught here in an air bubble, trapped in a metal entrail of the city. "Angela," I sobbed openly, "are we going to die?" I threw my arms around her, clinging to her like a child.

"Calm down now," Angela said soothingly, controlling her fear.

Then came the piercing announcement of our death sentence. "DIE … DIE … DIE," a hideous, screeching voice mimicked my last terrified word! Icy silence followed.

"A madman!" I whispered, and felt my blood turn to cider and my legs to cotton. I slid down into a sitting position, and Angela followed.

"Get control of your breathing," she directed. "That was only a harmless parrot squawking."

We sat there while each elastic minute stretched with growing tension. No one knew where we were. Angela's parents would not return for several days, and there was no one to help us.

Angela grabbed her umbrella, and I thought she was going to strike me. Instead, she shoved it at me and said excitedly, "Use the handle to make all the noise you can, Connie." And without question, I did.

In a moment, Angela took my hand and squeezed it hard. In three infinite seconds, the elevator purred and moved down, the light showing our regular descent. On the first floor, after another eternal wait, the precision doors parted to freedom.

Two men in sky-blue work clothes, with "Otis" stitched neatly in red on the pockets, stood there with stern looks on their faces. "What are you two poking around in here for? You could get yourselves into real trouble, breaking in like this," the shorter one said.

"We were just window shopping from the inside," Angela remarked with a glance at me and a toss of her blond hair.

"How did this happen?" I asked, feeling exhausted and elated all at once.

"We cut the electricity for about sixty seconds, and that is when you two came through the electronically operated doors without any help from the alarm. When we saw the elevator moving, we intentionally trapped you between floors. After listening, we knew you had just happened in, but decided to teach you a lesson. Our business was to fix a whine in the elevator. Now, get out of here, and don't come back until Monday morning."

"How did you know what to do, Angela?" I asked as we raced back to the car.

"I remembered the Otis truck we parked beside," she said. "Then I realized that if the lights in the elevator were on and the buttons, which are electric switches, would operate the elevator, someone could be controlling us from somewhere in the store. I hoped the noise would alert them."

"Let's go home, Angela," I said wearily, as we scrambled into the car.

"I would like to take you to the National Museum of Racing," she remarked, glancing at me sideways. "I don't think it is open, but you will probably find a way to get us in."

"That's not funny, Angela," I grinned sheepishly. And then I heard myself saying a strange thing. "There is plenty of time to see the museum tomorrow or Tuesday. Besides, I have a message for you from Wilton, and I need help in planning your party."

Angela maneuvered the car expertly into the merging traffic and followed the wet, shining pavement home.

Aunt Minnie's Farm: A Memory

We swung off the highway that wound through the countryside like a carelessly dropped ribbon and rattled onto the red-clay washboard road that led to Aunt Minnie's farm. This rough ride delighted us children; our '36 Ford shimmying, angling like a trotting dog, coils of pink dust boiling out behind.

Deep gullies on either side formed a bridge of sorts that transported us into the past — or, at least, the recent past — and the August sun, like a livid cannonball, aimed itself directly at the intruders who dared to cross it and disturb the drowsing farm.

Ahead, we saw the patch of trees that protected the sturdy, spacious house, built in the '20s and wrapped halfway around by a wide, welcoming, vine-covered porch.

Great oaks, like angels of mercy, spread their leafy fingers in a blessing of shade. Their toe-like roots, looking like claws with their bent knuckles angled sharply, strained for a footing in the brick-hard earth. But even the shade was sweltering, and the entire farm seemed to have settled restlessly under the humid breath of a yawning universe.

As we pulled into the yard, enveloped in a cloud of dust, Sheba the shaggy brown-and-white collie greeted us with the sound of hoarse, hollow barking, her busy tail a metronome to the lullaby world. Presently, she sat at attention, her thick, pink tongue limp and lolling to one side and dripping perspiration; her watchful eyes, set in a sensitive slant, rolled about, delighted with this break from boredom, for she had lost interest in her favorite game of ruffling the chickens.

Usually voracious in their scratching, the hens had stumbled in their tracks, beaks open, throats pulsating, red eyes rolled back in their heads, mesmerized by the oppressive heat. Even the bees droned in a slower, lowered key as they fidgeted about the stricken clover.

Beyond the yard and prized smokehouse lay a cluster of pecan trees, and farther still spread the apple orchard. Its humid air, like a greedy sponge, hoarded the smell of the rotting, soured apples that peppered the ground.

Behind the house and barely visible from the highway, the tired barn squatted in a patch of trees, exhaling earthy, pungent odors of horses, hay dust, harnesses and rusting tools. Nearby the sagging wagon rested in the shade with its tongue grounded, its unsteady wheels weighty with sleeping creaks and promising to creep a snake-line down the pine-cradled road.

Directly in the center of the yard stood the covered well. The rickety, temperamental pump handle, poised like a conductor's baton, squeaked out a symphony of sounds that perhaps inspired Mother Earth, for the crystal-clear water gushed bubbling and churning, frothing and dancing from the pipe as it splashed into the bucket, droplets zinging. This artesian water, so cold that we called it liquid ice, was gulped from cooled gourds causing our eyes to water and our stomachs to rebel in pain.

The screen door slammed like a trap as Aunt Minnie set down a frosted pitcher of tart lemonade and wafer-thin sugar cookies. She was a tall, bony woman — strange that I always remember her talking to me at eye-level — and when she hugged me long and hard, I could feel her old bones poking their way right into my heart.

Poems from the Heart

Birth of Spanish Moss

Nature held her apron wide,
Gathered gray froth from the tide;

Caught the grandeur of the ocean,
Snared a stray and graceful motion;

Fashioned tangled strands that blow,
Kissed by sun and moonbeams glow;

Chased the melody from rhyme,
Teased enchantment from all time;

Spoke her magic incantation,
Swayed with rhythmic undulation;

And with apron wide she tossed
A lacy veil of Spanish moss.

Ode to the Elderly

Thank you, Lord, for glasses
That help me see aright,
And thank you for my dentures
That give a perfect bite.

And thank you for the makeup
That hides the wrinkles on my face;
And, Lord, thank you for the screws
That hold my hip in place.

And thank you, Lord, for caring for the birds,
But frankly, Lord, why can't they manage alone?
Then you could come much faster
When you hear me cry and moan.

And thank you for my good memory,
Though I must in honesty say
I just took out the chicken
I cooked day before yesterday.

Lord, I know I'm not quite perfect
And not all that I should be,
But couldn't you forget the birds
And spend more time with me?

Lord, sometimes I think I'm ready
To come and live with you,
But please don't send heaven's bus today
'Cause I'm shopping the mall with Thelma Lou.

So when my life is old and spent,
Lord, promise me Your care,
So if I die in some bad accident
I'll be wearing my best pink underwear.

I know my thinking's narrow, Lord,
But I really hope you'll see;
You oughta forget that sparrow
And keep your eye on me!

Prayer/Thoughts for Israel

O how God loves Jerusalem, the sacred city, the navel of the earth,
The apple of God's eye.

God has chosen His people from all the peoples of the earth,
Not for anything they have done —
But because He, He Himself, has set his love upon them.
Like a mother tending a wayward child,
He has drawn them back time and time again to Himself,
Sometimes allowing them to experience the pain of their rebellion
because of His overwhelming love.

May the enemies of Israel perish!
May the hatred in their hearts and the weapons in their hands
Boomerang a Davidic vengeance upon them.
May the enemies' rockets veer wild in the wilderness,
Sparing even the meanest shrub and the least of the forest creatures.

May the fear of the children be as flint to their bones;
And may they grow, mature and proliferate
as their forefathers in the wilderness.
May hunger flee to the hills and pain perish in the beloved sea.

May emigres soar safely to their new homes on wings of eagles,
their Aliyah another fulfillment of prophecy.

May the desert bloom
with blinding and riotous colors:
Gauntlet greens, defiant reds —
Screaming out the blessings of God
Upon Holy Israel
To the surrounding jealous nations.

And may God dance in delight
Over His people;
And ring out an eternal reverberating blessing
Upon each chosen one.

Selah.

A Greater Thing

Glorious and good is our God,
Mighty and merciful is He;
He wings across the mountaintops
And walks upon the sea.

He scatters glittering jewels by night,
Guides the burning ball by day;
Hurls lightning bolts that crack the night,
That gives me pause to pray.

He churns the ocean's seething tide,
Its fragrance deep and wild;
He awakens the grumbling volcano's blast,
Then thunders through the mountain pass,
While hailstones rain on stormy heights
Unveils the moon to awe the night.

Yet a greater thing than these He's done —
Hallelujah! Praise God! He gave us His Son!

Zacchaeus

(Luke 19:1-10)

Zacchaeus, Zacchaeus, oh what a reputation!
Only Jesus could bring consolation,
To a name so drenched in forward fame,
To a name so drowned in scandalous shame.

A little man, dark-eyed and cunning,
Traitor to his Jewish birth, how stunning!
No longer a son of Abraham,
More a fox and not a lamb.

Chief of tax collectors, chief of sinners,
Loveless and lost, as cold as the winters.
The people despised him and were quite numb
To what Zacchaeus might one day become.

Of the choicest morsels he did partake,
Dressed in the finest for vanity's sake.
Though nimble and quick in body and mind,
Yet plainly withering on the vine.

Zacchaeus, a mind and heart full of greed,
Oblivious to his prodigious need.
Lacking compassion, humility and mirth,
He had never heard of the second birth.

On his little finger, a ring he wore
And often thought that he was more
Than the common man who passed him by,
And heard not their need or painful cry.

Yet humbling his dignity, he climbed the fig tree,
Jesus! A sudden gripping urge to see!
Then Zacchaeus heard the most compelling sound;
It was Jesus calling Zacchaeus down!

"Zacchaeus, come down now.
I must stay at your house today."
So Zacchaeus immediately shimmied down
And felt a strange excitement round.

The brightness of Jesus' glory burst forth from His eyes;
In himself, Zacchaeus saw the arrogance, the greed, the pride.

His surprised self-recognition broke Zacchaeus' heart
As Jesus dropped the saving seed into the broken part.

Then Zacchaeus dared to gaze deep into Jesus' soul,
Saw the oceans of love more precious than his hoarded gold.
His spirit blossomed like a white, twining rose,
A new and joyful man from his head down to his toes.

The righteous ones were aghast and grumbled
Not seeing that Zacchaeus was so beautifully humbled.
Blind to a pagan becoming a lamb
And now a true son of Abraham!

"Lord, Lord! Here and now I give
Half of my possessions to the poor;
And if I have cheated anybody out of anything,
I will pay back four times the amount."

Because Jesus had saved him from out of the pit,
The name he had now undeniably fit.
All Zacchaeus' sins, through Jesus, were wondrously undone;
Zacchaeus, his name and person now matching, means: "The just one."
Zacchaeus, Zacchaeus, oh what a name!

The Ten Lepers

(Luke 17:11-19)

In solitude, Jesus walked the dusty way
Toward a little village where He planned to stay.
He was quite weary but took no care
For He knew He had a mission there.

Calling out to Jesus were ten leprous men;
Many presumed them racked by sin.
The Jews thought lepers mirrored God's displeasure;
But God saw them as an opportune treasure.

Loudly, they called, "Jesus, Master, have pity on us!"
Not asking for healing, but for what Jesus thought just.
In respect, the nine lepers were precisely the bottom,
Yet the Samaritan was lower as if from Sodom.

"Go show yourself to the priest," Jesus said,
And in going they were healed from their toes up to their head.
Yet only one returned, praising God loudly,
Giving himself to Jesus both humbly and proudly.

All his love to his Lord to greet

Throwing himself at Jesus' feet.

The nine were healed by Jesus' compassion and power;

But the Samaritan, by faith, being saved that hour!

The Widow of Zarephath

(1 Kings 17:7-16)

Old and forlorn the widow cried
With pent-up pain she could not hide,
And her steps were heavy as her heart
For she and her son, life soon must depart.

All her dreams had vanished or burst;
It seems as though her life were cursed.
A little meal, a little oil,
All that was left of her life of toil.

Her tortured fingers, like the sticks she found,
Were old and gnarled, as she culled the ground.
A little fire she would make;
A little bread she would bake.

Soon in her arms she would mourn her son,
They would eat their last meal, then life would be done.
She would hold him tightly to her breast,
Dying in pain and longing for rest.

Startled, she heard the prophet's cry;
Bring me water and bread that I might not die.
Her eyes were dim and hardly seeing
As she groaned within her spirit being.

Aggrieved, she said, as the Lord your God lives,
I have no loaf but a handful of meal
And a little oil. I'm gathering sticks that I
May bake for me and my son that we may eat bread and then die.

And Elijah answered her: The Lord,
The God of Israel says, "The jar of meal
Shall not waste away, or the bottle of
Oil fail until the day that the Lord sends rain."

Struggling to accept this grand revelation
There fell upon her a heavenly jubilation.
Joyfully she went quickly for the water and bread,
Now so alive when once she was dead!

Her spark of faith brought salvation and grace
And, oh, what a change in her fingers and face!
As the grain and oil multiplied,
Hope for her son and herself was realized.

And the three of them feasted that very night
On fresh bread and olive oil with joy and delight.
And their voices they would often raise,
Giving thanks to God in glorious praise.

And Elijah taught them from the sacred writings
Of Abraham, Moses and the coming good tidings.
And Elijah loved the little fellow
Who often rested upon his pillow.

Life to them now a precious treasure
And God bestowed peace and hope beyond measure.
So the Lord blessed them in all their ways
And Elijah dwelled with them many days.

Rachel and Leah

(Genesis 29 and 30)

When Rachel had no children,
And Leah had no love,
Rachel went to Jacob,
Leah to God above.

And because Leah was unloved,
Some thought it unscientific,
That somehow she did manage
To become somewhat prolific.

Leah boasted of her four children:
Reuben, Simeon, Levi and Judah.
And Rachel became quite jealous
When Leah would toot her tooter.

So Rachel went to Jacob,
"Give me children or I die!"
"Don't get mad at me," said he,
"God's in charge, NOT I!"

So Rachel gave him Bilhah;
Jacob was happy as could be.
And when he saw his baby Dan,
Said, "Wow, he looks so much like me!"

Now Bilhah made Rachel jealous.
She said, "Jacob, stop this dally!"
But her warning came too late,
For out popped lil' Naphtali.

But this unsettled Leah,
Truly a competitive dame.
So she gave Jacob Zilpah,
"We, too, can play that game!"

So after the game was over,
There appeared this one named Gad.
Jacob and Zilpah were happy,
But it just made Rachel mad!

Again, with Zilpah the game was played
And Rachel made a jealous dash

When she saw Leah's tiny newborn,
The pair had nicknamed him Ash.

So Leah bought her husband,
And love apples were the price.
She gave birth to baby Issachar,
But still not a happy wife.

Though unloved, Leah had another son,
Jacob's honor she hoped to earn.
When Rachel saw Zeb, their precious new one,
She stomped out the door with a jealous heartburn.

At last, Leah got her druthers,
Little Dinah made happiness abound;
For now her older brothers
Had a sister to kick around.

Then God remembered Rachel's plight;
Jacob gladly did comply.
And to them a handsome son was born —
Joseph, the apple of Jacob's eye.

Then Rachel bore another son.
Said she, "Benjamin's from Jehovah!"
Then Jacob, at last, had a chance to speak.
Said he, "I think my game is over!"

Now if your family's a muddle, dear,
Ungracious, rude and unpunctual,
Just remember Rachel and Leah,
Whose home was truly dysfunctional.

Even so, Joseph, Rachel's son, saved many lives
And what an example of how to live!
Had one, not several wives,
And taught his brothers to forgive.

From Judah's lineage, Leah's son,
Came the most prophetic one.
He paid the most exorbitant price,
To forgive our sins and make us right.
None other than
Our Lord and Savior, Jesus Christ!

And if your family is truly a mess,
Just go to Jesus and truly confess.
He will transform your home,
Make it sweeter than the honeycomb,
And give you the needed rest.

The Crown of Thorns

Jesus wore the crown for me,
The crown of thorns that set me free;
The weight of sin upon His breast
Brought precious peace and perfect rest.

A crown of long, sharp thorns was made,
Upon the Savior's head was laid.
Deformed hearts with twisted bent
Could not bear the innocent.

Soldiers stripped off the clothes He wore;
They gawked and laughed and plotted more.
A purple robe on Him was laid;
In ignorance, Jesus' divinity, displayed.

With reed, they smote that sacred head,
Stumbling and staggering He freely bled.
Mocking Jesus, they bowed the knee,
Hailed Him with Satanic glee.

While thorns pierced His scalp and cheek,
The Lord submitted bowed and meek.
Blood and sweat mingled down,
While trembling angels hovered 'round.

They struck with fists and slapped with palm;
No hope for Him, no heaven's balm.
Soldiers reveled, and with joy they looked
At the fiendish blows our Master took.

They spat on Him with putrid breath,
Excited by His coming death.
Tears of forgiveness flowed down His face,
Without one soul to plead His case.

Jesus wore the crown for me,
The crown of thorns that set us free.
What did we sinners receive instead?
A crown of glory for our head! *(Psalm 8:5)*

I ask you, friend, if you were there,
Would you be one to jeer or stare?
Perhaps you believe down in your heart
That you would not have taken part.
But if you claim you truly care,
You know that you were really there.

Jesus Turns Water into Wine

(John 2:1-12)

The third day, Jesus came to Cana of Galilee,
Performed a miracle also for you and me.
The occasion was a marriage, a time for joyful celebration,
As had been throughout the nation for every generation.

For the gloriously, jubilant, happy pair
Who shone like stars free from care.
And the sky graced them with the brightest star,
But God outshone them with HIS Son, by far.

And the luscious food, oh, what a spread!
Just as it should be for those who wed.
And the wine, how generously it flowed
For all those invited to the adorned abode.

Jesus, Mary, and the disciples came.
Jesus, without fame or miracles to His name.
The beautiful festival long continued without fanfare,
Love, affection and fellowship greatly flourished there.

Then, an obstacle rumored, quite contrary,
But believed and acted upon by Mary.
She said to Jesus, "They have no more wine,"
Perhaps expecting from Him a sign.

Jesus asked, "Woman, why do you involve me?"
Calling her woman, showing no partiality.
Jesus lovingly rebuked Mary, for it was not yet His time,
And unknown to Mary, the vats still held some wine.

Delays of mercy are often not denial,
But may seem hard as though a painful trial.
And Mary said to the servants, "Do what He tells you,"
And the servants did just what she said to do.

They filled with water six stone jars to the brim.
Jesus' mother's hope grew perhaps confused or dim.
Then Jesus said, "Take some to the master of the banquet,"
And the servants immediately took it to him.

The master of the banquet was shocked
At how the wine in the water was unlocked.

So thankful that He was saved from embarrassment,
Perhaps from sly remarks or even harassment.

Jesus came to grace and bless them,
And He will meet our need if we let Him.
But if we truly want His care,
We must ask for His presence in daily prayer.

Jesus Quells the Storm

(Mark 4:35-41)

Jesus said, "Let us go to the other side."
The disciples with Jesus were happy to oblige.
But they had no vision that their lives someone must save.
If they were not to go down to a watery grave.

Suddenly, as Jesus fell asleep at the helm,
Peaceful and content within His kingdom realm,
A vicious, dangerous squall was born,
Leaving the disciples frightened and forlorn.

Hugh waves crashed against the distressed vessel,
So severe, no sails or oars could wrestle.
Forgetting that Jesus was by their side,
Their prowess as fishermen melted with their lofty pride.

The angry, swirling winds howled over the stern,
So much so, they feared the boat would overturn.
"Master, Master, don't You care that we drown?"
The disciples were sure the ship was going down!

Jesus slept to test their faith and prayer;
And the sinful disciples thought Jesus did not care.
Against their Lord's kingdom the men committed treason,
For their foolish fear had overwhelmed faith and reason.

Jesus' body slept, but His heart was fully awake,
And His resting body did not His power take.
A tortured ship could never sink,
For Jesus is our saving link.

Jesus' word of command rebuked the storm —
"Quiet! Be still!" the wind and waves collapsed their form.
And as a newborn baby falls asleep,
A blissful peace and hush fell upon the deep.

Jesus reproved the disciples: "Why are you so afraid?"
Where was their foundation Jesus so carefully laid?
And when our sea is tossing, we must "be still!"
For with Jesus at the helm, the storm can do no ill.

Jesus Heals a Leper

(Matthew 8:1-4)

Many there came to hear Jesus speak,
The proud, the rebellious, a few who were meek.
Many hearts were much amazed,
But few hearts were set ablaze.

For most hearts were dark or dim
Without godly desire to cling to Him.
But a small remnant came in humble participation,
Returning Jesus' love with heartfelt adoration.

Some saw leprosy as from the hand of God
That struck evil with power, like the shepherd's rod.
Never thinking that Jesus' hand
Could cure a leper or any man.

And never thinking any higher,
Unable to imagine Jesus as Messiah.
But the leper came with healthy lust,
Knelt before Jesus sincerely with trust.

"Lord, if You are willing, You can make me clean."
Assured of Jesus' power, a faith not often seen.
And with a humble submission to Jesus' will,
No matter what Jesus' answer, he would love Him still.

Jesus reached out and touched the loathsome limb.
"I am willing, be clean," Jesus spoke to him.
And immediately the joyful leper was cured,
Losing memory of the horror he had so long endured.

Jesus healing him was not in stone set,
But issued from a humble request that Jesus gladly met.
And Jesus said He would,
Because the leper believed He could!

A few seeing the miracle were now convinced,
Jesus heals immediately without recompense.
And Jesus heals our sin, the leprosy of the soul;
Sin corrupts completely and takes a devastating toll.

Jesus lovingly commanded,
"Don't tell anyone.

And go show yourself to the priest;
And offer the gift Moses commanded."

Jesus wanted him to be seen,
So the priest could declare him completely clean.
Are we completely clean? We must do our part
And allow Jesus, our High Priest, to look into OUR heart.

Jesus Walks on Water

(Matthew 14:22-33)

In their boat, Jesus sent the disciples away,
While He went up the mountain alone to pray.
Jesus prayed till the fourth watch of the night,
Yet still the darkness hid the light.

The disciples were in the boat far from land.
The voyage was fair at first, but now they need a saving hand.
For suddenly the night turned ferociously stormy, surprising them there,
While the Lord labored in deep and zealous prayer.

In the beginning the disciples felt little doubt,
Because Jesus is the one who sent them out.
They sailed forward in the storm, changing not their tack.
The disciples trusted Jesus and did not dare turn back.

But now the violent wind and waves convulsed the boat.
The men were wildly fearful that they could not stay afloat.
Why had Jesus sent them into the storm,
To panic them and leave them there forlorn?

Jesus stepped out, the waves humbled themselves at His feet;
And Jesus glowed as He walked serenely across the deep.
The terrified disciples thought Him an apparition,
But it was the Lord Jesus on His saving mission.

The disciples screamed in dreadful fear,
Not remembering the gracious Lord walks ever near.
Claiming to have faith, we must first be tested
To recognize the One in whom our faith is invested.

Sometimes we allow our hearts to be shattered to dust,
When Jesus is standing right there beside us.
Jesus, in compassion, spoke, "Don't be afraid. It is I."
Now their fear rested when Jesus drew nigh.

Peter spoke, "If it is you, Lord, tell me to come walking on the water."
Jesus said, "Come." Peter stepped out gingerly but did not loiter.
Peter wisely waited for an invitation,
For dangerous ventures truly need confirmation.

So courageous Peter walked miraculously upon the lake,
But the roaring winds his courage did forsake.

"Save me, Lord," the now-sinking Peter shouted
As his courage failed and himself he now fully doubted.

Peter, at first, had bold faith and zeal,
And walked upon the water until
He forsook Jesus' face and focused on the howling wind.
And now had only himself on whom to depend.

Jesus reached out and caught him
As He does with us when hope grows dim.
"Oh, you of little faith. Why did you doubt?
"Have I not taught you what faith is all about?"

Into the boat, Jesus and Peter climbed;
The disciples now perceived Jesus supremely exalted and divine.
The winds on the lake and in their hearts did cease,
And there fell upon them a heavenly, euphoric peace.

They joyfully gave Jesus the adoration due Him,
For now they believed they really knew Him.
Worshipping and exclaiming,
"Truly You are the Son of God!"

Jesus Heals a Sick Man
(John 5:1-15)

Up to Jerusalem! Up to the Feast!
All Jewish males from the strong to the weak.
But to the pool of Bethesda Jesus went,
To heal an invalid was His loving intent.

The blind, the lame, the paralyzed, too,
Oh, how pitiful for Gentile and Jew!
Suffering appallingly day after day,
With no caring soul their hope to convey.

An angel stirred the water at times,
But many lay there who were wholly resigned.
For they could not into the water step first,
And felt their lives had been woefully cursed.

Healing came when the water was in motion,
And, oh, how that thought should stir our devotion.
For most of us have blessed good health;
What a godsend it is, much more than wealth!

There lay a man for thirty-eight years,
And God had counted and bottled his tears.
Jesus fastened His eye on the weakest,
The one who had suffered the most and the deepest.

Not the soul's agent but a burden instead,
His poor self lay wasted from his feet to his head.
Sometimes in dreams he saw his body made right,
But his dreams melted like snow in the soft morning light.

"Would you like to get well?" Jesus inquired.
When the water is stirred, I'm too slow and too tired.
"Get up! Pick up your mat and walk," Jesus said.
So he shot to his feet and picked up his bed!

The lame man's body was transformed with health;
Jolted by joy, oh, what emotional wealth!
Muscle and sinew and life in him surged;
Delirious with laughter, his heartache now purged!

The Jews spoke, "It's Sabbath, put down that bed!
It's illegal, you know, but you're ignorant," they said.

It was zeal for the Sabbath the Jews pretended,
Their true desire to kill Jesus, God quickly upended!

And many there were who did not believe,
For a miracle by Jesus they could not conceive.
Evil cannot fathom the beauty of grace,
Just stares at it dumbly with a frown on its face.

Praising God loudly, the man flew to the temple,
Jesus found him and gave a warning so simple:
"Sin no more, for if you do,
Something worse will happen to you!"

The man's infirmity had interrupted his sin,
And that is why Jesus gave a warning to him.
Jesus completed his salvation, body and soul,
The new man stood before Jesus now shining and whole.

We must keep our hearts diligently, open and still;
Be ready and quick to accomplish God's will.
And God should not have to woo or implore us,
To see marvelous miracles dancing right here before us!

The Canaanite Woman
(Matthew 15:21-28)

To Jesus the woman made her confession;
Her daughter was under demonic possession.
And the woman's heart was broken and bleeding;
A touch from Jesus was all she was needing.

"Lord, Son of David, have mercy on me!"
Not merit, but mercy, she knew held the key.
Jesus answers the woman not a single word.
He turned a deaf ear as if He had not heard.

Oh! How discouraged she must have felt,
A silence of pain Jesus had dealt.
But every prayer is not answered immediately,
And often must be prayed for repeatedly.

The disciples wanted Jesus to answer her prayer,
But since He did not, they ceased to care.
"Send her away; she makes such a fuss.
Stop her from following after us!"

Jesus said, "I was sent only to Israel's lost sheep."
The woman was broken and began to weep.
It was a repulse and reproach Jesus gave!
She staggered under His words so grave.

But she worshipped Jesus and cried, "Sir, help me!
Please don't leave and then forget me."
"Bread for the children must not be fed to the dogs," Jesus said.
And with that, she stood and lifted her head.

To Jesus' hard word, she grew perplexed and mindless
And did not respond to His seeming unkindness.
Feeling that her hope now was dim,
She blames herself instead of Him.

"But even the puppies," said she, "eat the crumbs that fall,
And they are not grudged the crumbs at all!"
Faith finds encouragement even in loss,
And hangs on tightly whatever the cost.

This woman showed wisdom, patience and meekness,
Which overcame her heartbreak, fear and weakness.
But of all the graces, faith honors Christ most,
A work in a humble heart by the Holy Ghost.

"Woman, you have great faith," Jesus said.
Oh! How her soul rose up from the dead!
His words were like rain on a sun-parched earth,
And her heart exploded with rejoicing and mirth!

Jesus wanted her faith to prove,
And to a higher level her faith to move.
"Your request is granted." Her race was run.
He spoke, and it was immediately done!

A Canaanite woman, so lost and miserable,
Proved herself a true daughter of Israel!
We, too, have no merit on which to depend;
God's awesome grace only has grafted us in.

The Memorial Gift

(John 12:1-9; Matthew 26:6-13)

Simon, the healed leper, was the host,
Invited Martha, the homemaker, who knew the most
About making guests comfortable and at ease,
Cooking and serving with a kind heart to please.

And Jesus sat there with Lazarus beside Him,
Another sat there who soon would deny Him.
And Mary was there, who had once taken a seat
And chose the best part at Jesus' sweet feet.

Mary remembered the woman sinner
Who poured out the perfume on Jesus at dinner;
And how Jesus forgave her of all her sin
And sent her in peace a new life to begin.

Now Mary was given prophetic understanding
Of Jesus' soon coming death at God's commanding.
A pound of precious spikenard in an alabaster box,
She had kept it safe under key and lock.

So Mary broke open the box, spilling its contents,
The indignant disciples thought it foolish nonsense.
When she poured out the costly perfume on Jesus' feet and head,
They thought surely it should have been sold instead.

The disciples were thoughtless and needed teaching
But they truly loved Jesus and had grown from His preaching.
And they had repented and given their hearts to Him,
Even though their understanding was often quite dim.

But Judas Iscariot was the one most let down
And his face convulsed in an acid frown;
For his greedy heart was as black as his beard,
It was loss of the money for the bag he feared.

Anointing Jesus for His burial was Mary's holy purpose
The sweet smell so costly as she poured out the surplus
And seeing that Jesus was so graciously pleased
The disciples by their consciences now were seized.

Jesus was so gratified, He made it no mystery
That Mary's love gift would be remembered through history.
"The poor you will have with you always,
But I will be with you just a few more days."

Is the hoard in your alabaster box "just mine alone"?
Friend, who then is sitting upon the throne?
Remember, when on earth or to glorious heaven you've gone
God will reward abundantly those loving gifts you have sown.

A Nobleman's Son Healed

(John 4:46)

Jesus again came into Cana of Galilee.
There it was appointed for Him to see
A royal official whose son lay gravely ill;
And he needed Jesus his hope to fill.

Assaults of pain, of death, and sickness
Fall, too, upon the honorable, only sometimes for wickedness.
The official had such tender affection for his son,
He could have sent a servant, but he himself would come.

Jesus gave a mild rebuke even in the official's grief;
Knowing He would offer soon such grand and sweet relief.
Oh, you who need miracles, signs and wonders to believe,
For your faith so immature it cannot conceive.

If Christ smiles on us, He first frowns,
And if honest, we admit He has many grounds.
Jesus showed him his sin and then for him mercy prepares
And He will do the same for us, for we are beloved heirs.

He begged Jesus to come down before his son died;
It is right to petition, but not to prescribe.
He did not understand that Jesus did not have "to come down,"
For if his son died, Jesus, by natural laws, was never bound.

"You may go, your son will live," Jesus said;
Nothing Jesus spoke or did raised him from his bed.
"Not going down," Jesus did something better and faster,
Proving that truly He was Lord and Master.

The official took Jesus at His word and departed;
No sign or wonder, but he believes and is happy-hearted.
The servants met him with the amazing, awesome news;
There could be no deception, not even the slightest ruse.

For the patient was suddenly healed at the exact seventh hour,
Showing to each one the miracle was by Jesus' mighty power.
Believing in Christ's word, now believing in Christ,
Saved by Him alone, by His coming sacrifice.

The royal official went to Christ alone;
But brought his whole family salvation, joy never known.
Friend, are you experiencing Christ's frown?
Just ask, for His mercy forever abounds.

David and Abigail

(1 Samuel 25:1-42)

In the wilderness of Paran near Carmel Village,
The wealthy ranch owner, Nabal, owned sheep, goats and tillage.
He was exuberant in luxury, cheap in charity,
Noted was he for his vile rascality.

While in the wilderness, David's men offered a protective arm
For Nabal's sheep and goats and kept them from all harm.
Killing wild animals that could have raided the flock,
And with roving bands they did with swiftness block.

David sent ten hungry men with a modest petition,
For their needs were real and not just foolish fiction.
David's message to Nabal was as from a servant or son,
Not boasting about all the good for him they had done.

But surly Nabal denied and abused David's men,
Hurling insults despite how respectful they had been.
Hearing this, David's righteous anger was overcome;
As explosive rage seized him, striking him spiritually dumb.

"God curse me if one of his men remains alive!"
We will sting with vengeance like bees from a hive,
And by Satan, David was set on fire of hell.
No words his horrid temper could mend or veil.

This ragtag crew idolized David with an avowed bloody loyalty;
Dedicated to his protection, vastly esteeming his God-appointed royalty.
David furiously strapped on his sword with strength he had not known,
Revenge circulated through his heart and into his very bone.

Plundering time, David and his men thundered through the land,
With murder in their hearts and judgment in their hand.
As David slowed their pace descending a hill,
An image appeared, and though winded, made his heart stand still.

But Abigail's lovely face was but a firefly's glow to her spirit;
Her gracious, generous self, framed her lifelong lyric.
From her servants, she knew that David was understandably irate;
And death was surely the price with no debate.

Other words cannot tell of Abigail's magnificent appeal,
If one is humble, it will truly any marriage heal.

Dear Sister, read of how she made her humble plea
And pray God will grant her wisdom to you and me.

Abigail dismounted her donkey and humbly bowed low,
Wisdom is better than weapons, she wanted David to know.
For all the love on earth, all love is despite,
And she loved Nabal with compassion and godly insight.

"My Lord, let the blame be on me alone,"
And there rose up in her spirit a deep and heavy groan.
Abigail speaks passionately to David with deference and respect;
And with prudent, charming speech, she atones for Nabal's neglect.

"My husband is a selfish fool," Abigail said,
"But I am at your service to see that you're well fed.
Here's bread and roasted grain and choice cakes of raisins, too,
Wine and sweet cakes of figs all for your men and you."

"Bless the Lord God of Israel," David responded to Abigail,
"For without you, there would not have been left one male.
And if I had taken that evil dolt's life
The matter would have ended in bitterness and strife."

"Thank God for your goodly common sense,
And your gifted tongue to tame and convince."
David accepted the excellent provisions proffered;
"I will not kill your husband; go home without fear," he offered.

When Nabal, the next day, heard what had taken place,
He had a fatal stroke, collapsing forward, falling on his face.
What a miserable man with an evil-loving bent
And a devil's heart of stone that refused to repent.

When David heard that Nabal was dead,
He felt no sorrow, but praised God for justice instead.
Smitten first by Abigail's beauty, then by her God-fearing life,
David sent messengers to ask Abigail to become his wife.

In great modesty, Abigail yielded to David's request,
Knowing that David had no crown or throne as yet.
But Abigail was so moved by his teachable humility,
And into her heart, there flowed a joyful tranquility.

Quickly she prepared for the journey to meet her king,
Hardly considering she was moving from much to barely anything.

On her donkey and with her five maidens, she followed David's crew,
And with each step they took, her love for David grew.

The wilderness wind swept softly through the trees as they rode along,
And the maidens sang of David's exploits and feats in jubilant, glorious song.
Then David appeared, and Abigail's heart was drained of sorrow
As he gathered her in his arms, embracing her
with precious promises for tomorrow.

Who Is My Neighbor?
(Luke 10:25-37)

An expert in the law came asking Jesus a question.
Jesus expressed truths that should have brought confession.
But as to loving God, the expert would say no more,
As to loving his neighbor, he believed his a perfect score.

When the expert said, "You shall love your neighbor," he barred Gentiles.
Now Jesus must correct his prejudice and end his faulty wiles.
So He tells the man a parable of a Samaritan and a Jew,
And if he listens carefully, he will find out what he ought to want to do.

A certain businessman traveled down the Jericho Road,
With valuable merchandise in his purse, but not a heavy load.
Then thieves stole his precious goods and beat him 'til half dead
And left him with bloody wounds upon his limbs and face and head.

Fortunately, the heavens opened and there came a godly priest,
However, he was running late for a celebratory feast.
By the victim's cries and moans, he felt genuinely appalled,
But, regrettably, to this grand event he had first been called.

By God's grace, there came a pious and zealous Levite,
Angered by the victim's wounds, he deeply felt his plight.
And by this heinous deed, he was so offended
That he prayed briefly, but his plans could not be upended.

With utter compassion these two meant quite well.
The priest wanted justice and heaven heard him rail.
The sensitive Levite could not bear the sight of blood at all,
But both were sure someone else would answer his desperate call.

Then there came a despised Samaritan down the road;
His first thought to get the victim to a safe abode.
And his pity takes on a supernatural life of its own,
When he sees the poor man's bleeding and hears his woeful groan.

Washing and soothing the wounds with oil and wine,
He prayed for his healing to the One merciful and divine.
He bandaged his wounds from his own linen,
And prayed for those who had been abusive and sinning.

With the patient on his donkey, he walked along slowly
And in his spirit clearly heard the angels singing lowly.
And with kindness and compassion he took him to an inn
And paid two coins to the innkeeper on whom he could depend.

With tender words of encouragement, he bedded the man down
And promised to pay the extra cost the next time he came around.
And on his knees, he prayed for the man's healing and for the situation
That led to the privilege of helping and his heartfelt jubilation.

We were like that traveler, walking in spiritual death,
When Jesus, that good Samaritan, brought salvation's saving breath.
Are we like that expert who, behind his question, hid?
Or are we like the Samaritan and the loving good he did?

The Rose of Sharon

In a world so cold and barren
Grew the red-red Rose of Sharon.
From a root in dry ground springing,
Hope and joy, Salvation bringing.

The crimson Rose through heaven's gate
Provoked deep love or bitter hate.
The reddest rose on sin-lost earth
Came to give life, the second birth.

Healing diseases of every kind;
Brought new life to the deaf and blind.
Spoke a lame man from his bed;
Awakened Lazarus from the dead.

And for these marvelous, wondrous deeds,
There grew hatred, jealousy, demonic weeds.
Hideous tongues, horrid and spiteful,
Spewed vicious words vile and frightful.

Then the holy Rose was cruelly crushed
And from torn petals the red-red gushed.
Many there were who railed and scorned,
But few there were who wailed and mourned.

So with mighty power, God's grand design
Swept death to his dungeon, a prophetic sign.
The Rose of Sharon, blossomed once more
In splendid array as never before.

The Rose of Sharon, the awesome sacrifice,
Paid for our sins the ultimate price.
None other than God's own son,
Our Lord and Savior — JESUS CHRIST.

Nicodemus

(John 19:38-42)

Israel's esteemed preeminent teacher
Sought out the cosmos' supreme preacher.
Nicodemus came searching for Jesus by night,
Curious to learn and gain spiritual light.

Fanatically religious, but no closer to heaven
Than a loaf of bread with a pinch of leaven.
And even though he came with a desire to learn,
Clueless, his sinful heart must be overturned.

Because of Jesus' miracles, Nicodemus now believes,
But not that saving faith on which the Spirit breathes.
Believing that good works earn your salvation
Is denying that intimate, godly relation.

When Jesus said, "You must be born again,"
Nicodemus was jarred to his core and hardly could stand.
He understood symbolism and was not naïve,
But what he heard he simply could not believe!

If true, his own beliefs were but a façade
Of all he had learned and believed about God.
His pharisaical righteousness and biblical illiteracy
Were contrasting and contradictory to Jesus' true ministry.

Nicodemus from the Old Testament ought to have known
Salvation is by grace through faith alone.
The bronze serpent and Moses, Jesus patiently reminded,
And marveled that Nicodemus had been so blinded.

Upon hearing that Jesus loved the world, not just the Jews,
His ego was shattered with this unthinkable news.
Flailing and writhing under Jesus' loving assault,
Knowing not with Jesus' blood he had been bought.

So, stunned, he simply walked silently away,
But the seed Jesus planted bore fruit one day.
Nicodemus encouraged the Pharisees to keep their own laws,
But they viciously denounced him without just cause.

When Jesus died and hung still on the cross,
His followers despaired, all hope was lost.

But the Sabbath was coming and no time to waste;
Jesus' body must be tended, and that with great haste.

Pilate gave Joseph permission to take Jesus down,
And Nicodemus was waiting there, just to be found.
Joseph's and Nicodemus' hearts, once darkened with vices,
Humbly and lovingly wrapped Jesus' body with spices.

Oh, to be there on that dark, dismal day;
In that cold, rock-hewn tomb where their Master lay.
But soon He would burst forth from His unlawful demise,
And hundreds would see Jesus — with their very own eyes!

Ode to Marion

I miss you, oh, how I miss you.
Only words now can embrace
The beauty of your being,
Your godly, manly face.

I miss you, oh, how I miss you.
The golden voice you aired,
Like words wrapped in an old love song
That told how much you cared.

I miss you, oh, how I miss you.
So enamored of your charms,
I know the angels envied me
As you held me in your arms.

The enigma of your smile
Lit a flame within my heart,
No person, trial or even hell
Dared split our love apart.

But an angel appeared that very night
And took you by the hand,
And off you went — in glory, sent —
Into the promised land.

When you left me all alone,
It tore my life apart.
Our home, a house now empty
And I, a broken heart.

I miss you, oh, how I miss you.
The rocking chair is empty,
The table now for one,
The doleful day is dipping into the setting sun.

No footsteps down the walkway,
No hand upon the door,
No sweet call from the kitchen
From the one whom I adore.

Each day slinks backwards
Where all past times are stored,
Stealing bits of memories
Into its selfish hoard.

Then somewhere —
In the black hole of space,
God saw my writhing,
The smeared tears on my face.

And now, praise God,
I've been given just a taste,
In a shining, glowing bubble
Of God's comfort and His grace.

www.ingramcontent.com/pod-product-compliance
Lightning Source LLC
Chambersburg PA
CBHW060900090426
42738CB00022B/3479